THE
AUDACITY
TO CARRY ON

Abiding Love Stories

June Samuel

ISBN 978-1-68526-263-1 (Paperback)
ISBN 978-1-68526-264-8 (Digital)

Covenant Books
11661 Hwy 707
Murrells Inlet, SC 29576
www.covenantbooks.com

To Rosabelle, my mother
and
Captain Azariah, my grandfather

Instructions for living a life: Pay attention.
Be astonished. Tell about it.

—Mary Oliver

INTRODUCTION

Our stories, woven in different tapestries with different characters, share similar universal human traits and common behavioral patterns. Studies in neuroscience have shown that when the stories shared resonate with us, they can activate the data processing sensory centers in our brains, leading to an increase in the hormone oxytocin and leading to more empathy, bonding, and building human connections.

The people in our life stories, who touch and influence us in profound ways, become a part of us forever. When times are difficult and we want to almost give up on everything, their memories ignite that spark of audacity within. We somehow carry on, creating a more meaningful life for ourselves while honoring their legacies.

BEGINNINGS

Emily remembered asking her mother if she ever wished she'd never met her father. Her mother had said, "How could I ever regret anything that made you? Life is full of miracles and tragedies. We decide which is which and who we become because of them."
—Ruth Cardello, *Always Mine*

Mari's story begins in the middle of Rose's story.

The birth of a child is a monumental event in the life of a woman. Her rebirth in many ways.

The skies opened, and thus commenced a glorious show of hailstorm, with flashes of silver lightning strikes and roaring thunder. The crystal hail balls came crashing down from the heavens above, almost shattering the glass windows of the small hospital room in Southern India.

The woman in labor was waiting to get it over with. The fragrance of fresh jasmine flowers, still adorned in her hair, disseminated and filled the air. The nurse who came into the room gently and firmly scolded her, "Rose, didn't I ask you to remove all the flowers?"

Rose slowly removed the strands of fresh jasmine stuck to her long and thick dark hair. The young doctor, who followed the nurse into the labor and delivery room, examined her and said, "You are dilated about eight centimeters. It won't be too long."

Rose seemed surprised. "Not too long? From what everyone says about labor pains, I thought it would be more painful."

The doctor smiled and thought to herself, *This woman must be disassociating herself from her pain, and there is something unusual about her.*

Maya Angelou once said, "To describe my mother would be to write about a hurricane in its perfect power. Or the climbing, falling colors of a rainbow."

That description perfectly fit Rose. She was a force of nature to reckon with, always fiercely independent, was not really the marrying or nurturing kind. She was in her midtwenties, and her family was gradually increasing the pressure on her to get married.

She was not against the institution of marriage itself; it was just that she had not met anyone worthy of marrying, and she didn't have the urge or urgent need for a life partner and companion. She came from a family who greatly valued education; she had graduated from college with degrees in teaching and social work. She had an outgoing and talkative nature, and she could be described as an extrovert.

She also had an ability to make herself content in solitude; she was a happy loner with her varied interests and talents. Highly competitive by nature, she loved to play cards and chess, and she was very good at it. She relished beating her opponents, especially the men who were good players in a few moves. She had a passion to travel, and when the wanderlust took over, she traveled alone, mysteriously disappearing from time to time.

After graduation, her job search began, and her first real work opportunity was hundreds of miles from her home in Tamil Nadu. She applied for jobs in many places near and far, including the Grahams' home, built by Dr. John Graham in Kalimpong, overlooking the Teesta River near the Himalayan mountains.

For as long as she could remember, she felt a certain yearning to be close to hills and mountains. It gave her a sense of calm and peace when she was close to their vicinity. When the rare job offer came from the Grahams' home and she could be close to the spectacular tallest mountain peaks in the world, she readily accepted it.

The scenic sights, with the thick mist, looked like it descended from heaven above on to the majestic Himalayan mountains, and its beauty was breathtaking. Rose liked walking into the fog as the hard chill struck her skin. She enjoyed her work, educating young children from different parts of the world, and they were fond of her.

She was fearless with an abiding faith, and when troubled, she turned to the Bible and an old hymnbook she carried with her. There was a small chapel on the school grounds, which had services a few times a week. She had learned to play the piano from her mother, Nesa. Whenever they sang her favorite old hymn, "Oh Lord my God, when I in awesome wonder," she quickly volunteered to play the piano and sang along.

When she was occasionally homesick, she fervently wrote handwritten letters. It was the primary mode of communication in those times. An ardent and expressive letter writer, her handwriting was calligraphic, inviting, and made it pleasant to read them.

Life near the Himalayas lasted for a little more than two years. Her parents insisted that she return home to be married, as there were several good proposals. Rose reluctantly met with some of the potential grooms. She did not see anyone. She felt she could handle her free spirit until Sam showed up.

When she met Sam, it was not love at first sight. Sam was a simple and smart man who worked as a lecturer at a university. They met a few times by themselves. Rose was at ease with him, and he did not seem to mind her being herself. After a few months, they agreed to get married.

His personality was the exact opposite of Rose's. He was an introvert, quiet and reserved. He had grown up in a village near Kanyakumari, also known as Cape Comorin, in the southernmost tip of the Indian peninsula. It is a scenic place where the waters of the Arabian sea, Bay of Bengal, and Indian ocean merge, with spectacular views of the rising and setting of the sun.

Sam would go on weekends to see the sights, sit on the rocks on the beach, and watch the mighty waves crash on them from different sides and pull away. He felt that pull and dreamed that someday he could travel across these seas and oceans to distant lands. He was always an honor student and the first in his family and small village to attend college. The people in his family and village were proud and pointed to him as a model student.

The woman who loved the mountains met the man who loved the oceans. Sam was enamored by the enchanting Rose and was immediately under her spell. They were soon married, and she became pregnant. Sam lost his job when Rose was seven months pregnant. Rose returned to the home of her parents, as Sam restarted his job search. There was much uncertainty about their future.

A few hours had gone by, and Rose felt the cramps becoming intense and presumed that it could be the onset of the final phase of labor. The wavelike contractions were getting more frequent and stronger. The pain was still bearable, and the nurse had given her some medication to relax. She felt a little groggy. Her mind began to drift away, with visions of the majesty of the glistening silvery ice caps of the Himalayan mountains touching the blue skies.

She tried to softly sing the lines from her favorite song to herself, "I hear the mighty thunder, thy power throughout the universe displayed; Then sings my soul, my Savior God to thee, how great thou art, how great thou art!"

It was interrupted by the pressure and hands she felt on her perineum. "Come on, Rose. Push, push, you are almost there, almost done."

There was a pause, followed by the sweet sounds of a newborn's cry. "It's all over, Rose. See, here's your baby girl."

Rose felt relieved and glad that it was a girl. She was not eager to hold the baby, but the nurse insisted she did, so she took the baby and held her in her arms. The baby looked all right. She counted the baby's fingers and toes and saw that she had all ten. Her face looked bright, with a head full of dark hair and sparkling eyes. The long eyelashes had resemblances of her maternal grandmother, Maria, a phenomenal woman ahead of her times.

Her skin looked pink with a slight golden-yellowish hue to it, and she made an association to the appearance of golden-yellow marigold flowers, sunny and bright.

She gently whispered in the baby's ear, "Welcome, Marigold, to this big world."

CLOSE TO THE EDGE

Here's the deal. The human soul doesn't want to be advised
or fixed or saved. It simply wants to be witnessed—to
be seen, heard and companioned exactly as it is.

—Parker Palmer

It was a cold afternoon in November. Dr. Mari Sam was volunteering at the Suicide Prevention hotline. Her work schedule was hectic, but she wanted to volunteer. The phones would not stop ringing.

"Hey, Dr. Mari, you want to take this call?"

"Sure," she replied, picked up the phone, and said, "Hello."

There was barely anything said at the end of the other line. "Hello, are you there?"

After a long pause, there was a feeble voice. "Yes, I am here."

She could barely hear what he was saying.

"Can I help you? Are you all right?" asked Mari.

"I took some pills and don't want to go on no more," he replied.

Mari stayed calm. "How many? What kind of pills did you take? Are you okay?"

"I took Tylenol, maybe ten or twelve."

Mari was not sure if he was telling the truth. His caller ID number was showing up on her telephone screen, and she signaled to another volunteer to call 911.

"Are you sure? Do you want me to call 911?"

"No, nah." He seemed resistant. "I wanted to take more pills and end this horrible life, but that's all I had."

She continued to communicate, reaching out to him. "It's good you called this hotline. Can you tell me more about your situation and what is going on?"

"I lost my job, am broke, and have nothing and nobody. My girlfriend broke up and left me. I have nothing left to go on. No one really cares."

"Why do you say that no one cares?"

"'Cause no one does. I am going to hang up, got nothing to say, everything is falling apart." He paused.

Mari was trying keep him on the line, hoping somehow that he will continue to talk to her.

"Is your family around? Is someone there who can help you?"

"Nobody is here right now. I wanna be left alone. I am sick and tired of everything. I have hurt my mama so many times and broke her heart. She is having a bad time herself."

"What about your dad?"

He started cussing. "I don't want to talk about him, that ——" and he cussed more. "God knows where he is. You are beginning to annoy me, lady. I don't know who the hell you are, you and your weird accent. I don't understand half of what you're saying."

Mari thought to herself, *If he is noticing my accent, maybe he is paying attention to what I'm saying, and maybe I am getting through to him.*

"Just hang in there. Can you tell me your name? We can talk as long as you want to."

"Ya, it's Sean. How many times do I have to tell you to leave me alone? Why do you care?" he snapped. "Who put you on this line anyway? You can't even talk properly!"

Mari was trying to be careful, measured her words, not annoy him and get cut off.

"I would really like to help, Sean. You are not alone, you know."

"Oh yeah. This girl, we were so close to being engaged. She dumped me in my low point, so what's there to do now?"

They continued talking for some time until he said, "Wait, there is someone at my door."

"Sure, don't hang up on me, I'll be here. I'll be here as long as it takes."

A few minutes later, the voice of someone else came on the line, and it was not him.

"Hello, this is Officer Roy. Are you still there, ma'am?"

"Yes, I am."

"The young man seems to be okay. We are taking him to the hospital to be checked out. He will be coming to the Community Counseling Center in a few days, after he is checked out at the emergency room."

"Can I talk to him?" He gave the telephone to him.

"Sean, I'm looking forward to seeing you soon."

"Okay."

******

A few days later, Sean came over to the Community Counseling Center and met Mari for the first time. He was in his twenties, dressed casually, seemed a little disheveled, and had tattoos all over his neck and arms. He appeared to be calmer and more stable. He had been to the emergency room, where he was referred to a psychiatrist, and had started taking an antidepressant, which was prescribed.

"Hello, Sean, it's nice to meet you." He kept his head down as he sat on the chair. He removed his baseball cap and put it back on again.

"Hey."

"My name is Dr. Mari. Can you tell me a little bit about yourself?" Sean began to slowly open up at first, ranting and raving.

He suddenly became emotional; some tears rolled down from the corner of his eyes, and he wiped them with his right hand, which had a wound healing from a cut on his wrist.

Mari handed him a box of paper tissues. He looked at Mari and softly muttered to himself, "I am not sure why the hell I am here and talking to this strange Mexican woman."

Mari smiled and corrected him, "Well, I am Indian American, but does it really matter? We are here together, and we are going to try work together and make sure you are going to be okay. Life is hard, Sean. We must have the audacity to carry on."

Sean looked up at her, made eye contact with her for the first time. A smile creeped up, like he almost believed her. He seemed like he was willing to try and said, "I'll see you in two weeks."

After he left, Mari got a cup of coffee and relaxed for a few minutes.

She looked at the many framed pictures on the bookshelf, people who were and are dear to her. Among them was a large picture of an old man, smiling from a wooden frame with exquisite carvings. It was her beloved grandfather. She wondered what he would think of her now. As she closed her eyes and took a deep breath, her mind drifted to memories.

LEGACY OF GRAND LOVE

What was his creed? I do not know his creed, I only know
That here below, he walked the common road
And lifted many a load, lightened the task,
Brightened the day for others toiling on a weary way:
This, his only need; I do not know his creed.
His creed? I care not what his creed;
Enough that never yielded he to greed,
But served a brother in his daily need;
Plucked many a thorn and planted many a flower;
Glorified the service of each hour;
Had faith in God, himself, and fellow-men—
Perchance he never thought in terms of creed,
I only know he lived a life, indeed!
  —H. N. Fifer, "What Was His Creed?"

The high bamboo arches, at the entrance over the tall maroon iron gates, were covered with emerald green color creepers, which were bursting with pink, white, and purple Bougainvillea flowers. Some sticking and hanging out of them. As the gates opened, the small and beautiful garden became visible. A garden carefully planned and created to show off the beauty of nature in the glorious colors of flowers, shrubs, and trees. It was also created unknowingly to, perhaps, stir pleasurable memories in the future.

On the right side was a swing set, cast in tall stone pillars. A small slide and sand pit were added to complete the playground. On the left side was a water fountain with a circular wall with stone carvings, surrounded by foliage. The modest house painted in white was

17

the center piece, with windows painted in maroon color to match the gates.

To bring more life to the habitat, there were plenty of animals—birds, dogs, cats, rabbits, parrots, blue birds, and a small enclosed chicken farm in the middle of the huge vegetable garden, with all kinds of vegetables. There were also trees in the backyard, which yielded a variety of fruits: bananas, papayas, goas, and pomegranates to name a few.

It was the small paradise where Mari grew up, the home of her maternal grandparents.

It also felt like a sanctuary—welcoming—where warm hospitality was extended to anyone who entered its gates.

It is said that grandparents find ways to uniquely influence their grandchildren, and it also motivates them to live a more purposeful life and pass on their legacies. Mari was raised by her grandparents since her parents had to frequently move from place to place, continent to continent, due to the instability in her father's employment. They felt that she would be safe in the loving care of her grandparents, and it was a stable and healthy environment.

Mari was about three years old when her grandmother helped her wear the pretty pink dress and shiny silver *golusu*—anklets with hanging bells. She was delighted by the jingling sounds they made. She ran around the house, stomping her feet to make the sounds louder and louder. She wanted to show off her anklets to her grandfather. "Grandpa! Grandpa!" she screamed.

Her grandfather was working in the garden. When he heard her voice, he looked up and saw Mari standing at the edge of the stairs, coming down to the garden area. "Come down slowly, Marima. Be careful."

Step by step, she slowly went down the stairs but slipped and tumbled down the last two steps. A few bruises did not hurt much, but she started crying. "It will be all right, Marima. Get up and come to Grandpa. You must carry on, walk on the soil."

The soles of her small bare feet touched the wet muddy soil. It was soft and triggered strange feelings of comfort, as if she had returned to the familiar and safe ground which could not be explained.

It was perhaps the stimulation of the nerve points in the soles of the feet from which the energy forces flow through the meridians called *chi* or *qi* to the body's pathways and organs used in acupuncture.

Mari was especially attached to her grandfather, who was an extraordinary man. He was part of the greatest generation, a soldier who served as a captain with the British Allied forces in World War II. He was also well-educated and had worked in leadership and administrative roles in many institutions.

A lover of life with all its good and bad, he was a patron of the arts in all forms. He had great passion for literature in his native language, Tamil and English. He was fluent in both and taught literary courses in various colleges.

Those interests continued throughout his lifetime, and he immersed himself into scholarly research. He generously shared the data and information with other scholars and others with similar interests, who were exploring different world languages and literature.

He had the unmistakable aura of a warrior. He exuded strength with the heart of a humanitarian. It made people from all different backgrounds come to him in times of trouble. They fondly called him "Captain Sir." One of those rare people who was like a human rock of refuge, non-judgmental, and would not shun them in times of need.

He was a man of deep Christian faith and relentless optimism. He would try his best to help them, if he could.

His ancestors, six generations ago, had converted to Christianity. His personal faith did not stop him from being a true humanitarian. Christianity is a minority religion in India, a country historically with rich cultural and religious diversity. For the most part, it had been a relatively peaceful coexistence, with Indian Christians blending and reconciling local cultural traditions with Christian traditions. The common interests in language, arts, and literature made much in common to share as individuals.

He was not a perfect man and had his imperfections. He did not pretend to be holier than others and show off. He did not discriminate against anyone based on their religion, caste, socio-economic status, or other identity markers. And there was enormous personal respect for him. Mari witnessed him try his best to practice what he believed with authenticity, compassion, and conviction. Mari understood early in life, watching him and the people who came to see them, that humans are a complicated species with many shades. Every person is unique with multiple sides and dimensions.

Mari was his first grandchild, and he raised and treated her with absolutely no gender differences and exactly as he would have if he had a firstborn grandson. She was his constant companion and accompanied him to all kinds of places, and they met the most unusual people without fear and with an open mind.

He would often recite a few lines of his favorite poem by Rudyard Kipling, "If."

> If you can keep your head when all about you
> Are losing theirs and blaming it on you,
> If you can trust yourself when all men doubt you,
> But make allowance for their doubting too;
> If you can wait and not be tired by waiting,
> Or being lied about, don't deal in lies,
> Or being hated, don't give way to hating,
> And yet don't look too good, nor talk too wise:
> If you can dream—and not make dreams your
>   master;
> If you can think—and not make thoughts your aim;
> If you can meet with Triumph and Disaster
> And treat those two impostors just the same.

Mari memorized them and liked to recite them as well.

HOPE AND HEALING

The greatest mistake in the treatment of diseases is that there are physicians for the body and physicians for the soul, although the two cannot be separated.

—Plato

It was a warm and sunny day. The tropical heat had not completely taken over. Under the bright blue skies, the palm trees stood tall in perfect rows. The long green leaves shimmered and swayed gently in the afternoon breeze. The environment was tranquil and made it feel therapeutic, in an almost evolutionary way to reduce tension. The greenery was cooling to the eyes. The butterflies were busy flying around to the music of the chirping small birds.

Grandfather walked beside Mari as they walked the grounds of the hospital, where he served as a senior administrator. Mari was almost four years old and was beginning to gradually understand some parts of life as they began to unfold.

She saw people scattered all around. Some were all alone, and some are sitting in small groups.

"What are these people doing here, Grandpa?" she asked him.

"Marima, they are here to visit their loved ones who are sick and waiting for them to get better," he replied. Mari did not fully understand the word *sick*. Just that sick meant something was wrong with one's body and the inability to function well. She had a feeling that it was something deeper, more than the physical body itself and its dysfunctions.

There was a woman they knew with her children at a distance. She waved at them and gestured that she was coming over. Two of the children were older, and the youngest child was around Mari's age.

The woman looked concerned and said, "Ma was admitted two days ago in the hospital and is in critical condition, and I am worried, sir."

Grandfather comforted and encouraged her.

They talked for some time. Grandfather said, "We'll see what we can do to help with the medical bills. Don't worry about them now."

"We are staying in a hotel, sir, and they want us to move out today."

Without hesitation, Grandfather said, "You can all come and stay in our home with us, until your mother is discharged." There was a sense of relief in her eyes as she thanked him.

In her child's mind, Mari had a moment of realization. So many people are sick in this world need help and caring at this place, which is equipped to help them. She felt a sense of sadness and helplessness as they continue to walk.

"Who can help the people who are sick, Grandpa?"

He pointed to the sky and then to the people walking around in white coats with stethoscopes around their necks. "See those doctors and nurses."

There were women in starched white nurse uniforms and hats and men in white outfits, wearing small white caps, hurrying down hallways.

"Can we help them to feel better, Grandpa?"

He smiled and nodded silently.

"Do I have to wear a white coat to help them, Grandpa?"

"You can help them, with or without wearing a white coat, in different ways."

Mari was not fully convinced but believed whatever her grandfather told her for the most part. She adored and trusted him; he could not be wrong.

They walked to his office, where he picked up few small ivory color candles from the basket on his desk. Mari followed him to the small hospital chapel, which was not too far away. Before he entered the sanctuary, he lowered his voice and said, "We can also pray to the living God to help them heal and feel better."

The atmosphere of the chapel was solemn, extremely crowded with people in all the aisles. The sights of heavy hearts, silent tears, and pleading prayers were visible all around. In the middle of the altar, there was a huge wooden cross. On both sides of the altar, there were multiple small tables which had candles, some were burning and many stuck to it melted away in the shape of small and large teardrops.

Grandfather and Mari lighted the candles and placed them on the plates on the stand. They watched them brightly glow for a few minutes.

She was ready with her little folded praying hands and followed her grandfather's lead in saying a simple and short prayer she came up with all by herself.

"Did I pray correctly, Grandpa?"

"Yes, *Kannamma.*" he smiled and hugged her with one arm. *Kannamma* is an endearing term he used, which meant the one precious to me, like one's eyes and vision.

They walked outside and returned to the serene hospital garden. Grandpa tried to change the somber mood by pointing to the lovely flowers in bright colors all around.

"Marima, look at the yellow and white lilies blooming, and pink and red hibiscus blossom. Aren't they beautiful? They bring cheer to everyone without expectations. We should do the same, encourage and cheer up others and try carry on like them, no matter what."

Mari inhaled, taking it all in. She felt an ache and exhaled.

MISFITS AND OUTCASTS

Probably there is nothing in human nature more resonant with charges than the flow of energy between two biologically alike bodies, one of which has lain in amniotic bliss inside the other, one of which has labored to give birth to the other. The materials are here for the deepest mutuality and the most painful estrangement.
—Adrienne Rich

Rose visited Mari and her parents every few months, when she could, and wanted to see them. Sam had gone to Agra to complete his second master's degree in statistics and to increase his opportunities to get better work assignments. Agra was far away in the northern part of India, close to New Delhi, where the one of the architectural wonders of the world Taj Mahal was built by Shah Jahan as a monument in memory of his wife, Mumtaz Mahal.

And Rose was also back, pursuing her post graduate degree in education at another institution. All three of them were in different places.

Mari had completely bonded and was attached to her grandparents. She viewed her parents more like relatives, who visited them from time to time. She was cordial to them but did not like being with them or taking any instructions or advice from Rose. They pushed each other's emotional buttons, and Mari saw her as a dominating person, who was rude at times, and had mixed feelings about being alone with Rose.

Mari wondered why Rose was not like other mothers. She was not sweet and nurturing like them. She stood out as different. Her moods were unpredictable, and she was often demanding. One moment, she would be soft, like the petals of a rose flower, and the next minute, her prickly thorns would show.

Her grandparents always spoke well of Rose and Sam, trying to make her understand that they did not abandon her and loved her. There were no parents versus grandparents power dynamics with struggles, and they did not try to replace them or become possessive of Mari. In fact, they would constantly encourage and push her to spend time with Rose, when she visited.

"Be nice to your mummy. Be close to her." This made Mari really irritated at times and distance herself from Rose and avoid her if possible. They also had somewhat similar kind of high energy, like two alpha females; one adult and one child, which lead to clashing.

Their interactions mostly ended with a fight. Mari adamantly refusing to do what Rose told her to do. Sometimes, during her visits, Rose would take Mari out and spend the day with her, taking her to different places. Those outing days were tense and exhausting. Rose was hard to keep up with, and Mari could not wait to come back to her grandparents.

It was one of those outing days. Rose woke Mari up early in the morning. "Marima, wake up. It's your day out with Mummy."

Mari opened her eyes, stretched, and slowly got up. She was not excited. She showered and had a quick breakfast. Grandmother had made Rose's favorite breakfast, appams and fish curry. Rose liked seafood, and Nesa would make varieties of fish and shrimp dishes for her.

A small conflict started with the choice of clothes.

"Do you want to wear the red dress I bought for you, Marima?"

"No, no. I want to wear the blue frock Grandma bought me." Rose looked disappointed.

"Where are we going, Mummy?" Mari asked her.

"You just come with me. I'll show you."

Mari and Rose took the bus, and they came to the place next to a small hill with a fort, built on the huge rocks on top of it.

"We are going to climb this hill." Mari did not feel like going up the hill, it looked like a hard climb. "Say what, Mummy? I don't want to. Did you tell Grandpa you were taking me here?"

That pushed Rose's buttons, and her mood changed. "You are my child. I don't need anyone's permission to take you wherever I want to. I am different from your grandparents. They will dance to your tunes and do whatever you tell them do."

Mari didn't like that. She frowned and whined a little and followed her. There were a few men and small families in front and behind them. They were the only mother and daughter duo who were around.

The Vellore Hill Fort was built in the seventeenth century by the warrior Chatrapati Shivaji's army. Forts and old buildings built on hill and mountain tops were quite intriguing to Mari. She wondered how must have transported all the building materials and equipment up those steep hills. Did elephants and horses really carry them, or did they do it with building crane-like structures during those ancient times with their own ingenuity?

Halfway through, Mari was becoming tired. She grumbled and stopped walking.

"I can't climb anymore. Can we do it on another day?"

Rose looked at her and said, "We are almost done, almost there."

Mari sat on ground and refused to move, and Rose she felt a little sorry for her.

"Okay, let us go back down and get some lunch."

Mari was glad that she was not stubborn and make her do what she wanted to, as she sometimes did. They took another bus and went to another part of the town.

It was a popular restaurant. As they were about to order the food, Rose said, "You can order whatever you like, but you must order rose milk."

It was a chilled, sweet milk drink with rose flavor added to it. Mari really liked rose milk but did not want to give Rose the satisfaction that she listened to her.

"Why, Mummy, do I have to?"

Rose smiled and said, "Because it is named after your mummy. My name is Rose, and rose is my favorite color."

Mari found it amusing, she could not help giggling. The mother and daughter laughed together, as they occasionally did.

As they were about to leave after a sumptuous meal, Rose ordered many packets of mutton biriyani, a special preparation of rice made with various spices and goat meat. When they came out of the restaurant, she asked Mari, "Are you tired? Can you walk about a block? I want to give this food to some people."

Mari had rested by now, and she replied that she could.

As they walked to an area close by, there were a group of people who recognized Rose.

"Amma, you are back. It has been a long time."

Rose gave them the food packets, they seemed very happy. There were a few small huts nearby, and more people came outside to see them. Their appearances were slightly and noticeably different. She remembered what Grandfather had said some time ago. He had told Mari, when they came across others who had similar appearances, they had an ancient disease called leprosy. They sometimes stayed in groups and away from other communities. He said, "You should be sensitive and not be unkind to them."

It was the first time Mari was so close to a large group of people, who were openly stigmatized and were not part of mainstream society. She was not afraid of them.

As they were getting ready to leave, a few women in the group said, "When you come next time, please bring some clothes and sarees for us."

Rose replied, "I will."

They thanked Rose and asked her, "Who is this pretty girl? She looks just like you."

Rose seemed flattered and proudly said, "She is my Mari, my daughter."

It was a strange experience. Mari did not know what to think about her mother. She was surprised that she had been visiting the people they had just met. Rose apparently had some nice sides to her, although she did not show it often. She was her unique self and did not like to conform to imposed norms. It, perhaps, made her not want to get close to anyone, except for her husband, Sam. She felt freer with people who were different and unusual, those who were misfits and outcasts in society.

Rose said, "It is hot. We can go home now." Mari was ready to go home.

"We can go to a movie tomorrow. I heard that the new movie *The Sound of Music* is entertaining." There were mostly Tamil movies shown in theaters in that town, with occasional screenings of box office hit English movies and movies in other languages.

Since they were tired, Rose said she would find a taxicab, and they could return home soon.

As they were waiting, a white bird's feather came floating by and landed on the shoulder of Rose.

She was thrilled and exclaimed, "Ah, a white feather. It is from an angel's wings. It's always a good sign," and put it inside her handbag.

When they went home, Rose said, "Mari was a good girl today. She cooperated, and we only argued a little, not much."

Her grandfather seemed pleased. "That's good. Did you have a good time with Mummy, *Kannamma*?" Mari smiled, and she did not say anything.

She was slowly processing the strange day with her mother and various new experiences. It was overwhelming, and she did not feel like talking about it. She decided to keep it to herself, not make a big deal about it.

TO RUN OR NOT
TO RUN AWAY

I need to stop fantasizing about running away to some other life and start figuring out the one I have.

—Holly Black,
The Darkest Part of the Forest

The long school day had ended. Mari was in the third grade. It was time for her to go home, which was less than a block away. The smell of petrichor was in the air, and the tiny raindrops began to fall. Mari loved the rain. It was refreshing, and she wanted to get drenched for some time. There was no hurry, and she did not want to rush back home. Holding on to her small red umbrella, she jumped into the little puddles, splashing them with joy.

When she entered her home, her grandmother Nesa shouted at her, "Why are you late? It is raining hard. We are waiting for you, worried, and you have a surprise waiting for you."

Mari called Nesa *Amma* and replied, "*Amma*, why are you shouting at me, and why are you worried? You know I could not come running in the rain."

Ah, a surprise. Mari was excited, and her expectations were beginning to rise quickly. She placed the umbrella, dripping with water, down and wiped her face with the small towel her grandmother gave her.

As they went into to the living room, the surprise waiting for her turned out to be her friend Jaga sitting in her chair. Next to her was a small travel bag, full of clothes and a small pillow clumsily wrapped in a bedsheet.

Jaga had run away from home and had decided to move in with Mari and her family. They were both in the third grade but in different sections at the same school. Although they were from different backgrounds, they felt glad to be together and became friends. When it was lunch time, they sat under the big Banyan tree, opened their lunch boxes, and shared what they had brought from home.

Jaga always looked sad. She had dark circles under her eyes. She would become silent in the middle of a conversation and sometimes looked emotional, like she was on the verge of crying. Mari did not ask her why; she did not want to know. If they had a few minutes before classes, they went across the street to the small store. Mari always bought Jaga her favorite Cadbury's chocolate and Britannia biscuits. She always has some money with her.

It was Grandmother Nesa who taught Mari about saving money and the value of financial independence. She was careful about not being extravagant and tried to spend within her means. She always emphasized to Mari that a girl should always save, keep, and carry some money of her own with her.

If she needed money, even a small amount, she did not have to ask anyone and feel obligated toward them. She advised her that even she got married, she should save and keep some secret money for herself. Small amounts she could use and buy something she liked, without asking her husband or children every time for it.

One day, she showed Mari some of the money she was secretly saving.

"Are you going to buy something, *Amma?*"

"No, not now. I will buy something when I see something I like."

"What if you don't find anything you like?"

Grandmother said, "Well, then, I will give it back to the family if there is an urgent need. Once I save enough, I will put away some for my funeral expenses."

Mari did not understand what she was trying to say. Her grandmother continued, "When my mother, Mariammal, suddenly died, we did not have money for her funeral expenses. We had to go around looking for help, borrow from someone and pay them back with interest. I don't want that to happen to me. I don't want your grandfather to ask money for my funeral. It can happen in any family, even wealthy people. People fight over who has to pay for someone's funeral."

Mari did not know how to respond, but she could understand her Grandma Nesa better why she was always cautious and anxious about money. It made sense to her and thought it may be a good idea to be careful with money and follow her advice in money matters.

*****

Jaga said she was hungry. Grandmother Nesa made some fresh snacks; *vadais,* a tasty snack made with rice and lentil flour, served with coconut chutney and tea.

Mari's grandparents were calm. They did not make a fuss, and there was no drama. Her grandfather gently told Jaga that her family would be worried looking for her. Jaga started crying and said that she did not want to go home and wanted to stay with them. Mari did not know what to do. Grandfather went to Jaga's home and informed them that she was at their home.

Jaga's parents had four children, and she was the third child. To his surprise, Jaga's parents did not show much concern and said that it was fine with them, and she could stay with Mari as long as she wanted to. Grandfather told them that Jaga could only stay for a week with them, and he would then bring her back home to them. He then went to the local police station and informed the officers about what was going on. He did not want anyone to think that she was enticed or coerced to be with them against her will, and her family was aware of it.

Jaga was getting comfortable and attached to them. Her family did not make any effort to come and see her. Not even once. At first, it was fun having her around all the time. As time went by, it was becoming tiresome. She was becoming more and more moody and demanding.

Nesa tried to tell Jaga that everyone at their home was expected to do some small chores around the house. They were expected to remove their plates and cups after eating meals in the dining table and place them in the kitchen sink, but Jaga seemed indifferent.

Mari enthusiastically invited her to play with the pets and go around the garden, Jaga did not seem excited about it.

After a week went by and after many reassurances that she could visit them at any time, Jaga reluctantly went home.

It was an eye-opener for Mari. Every family is different, and not just hers, and they are not as they are portrayed in happy fairy tales. It was hard to see the reality that not every family would panic at the possibility of their child running away and not seeing them again. She presumed that all families would immediately search for them with enormous urgency and not let them go so easily.

She could not contemplate any thoughts of running away from home, for it may be really running away from life itself. She knew that if she was missing, her grandparents would frantically look for her. They showered her with unconditional love no matter what, in good and bad times.

It would deeply hurt them if she disappeared without telling them, and Rose would blame and fight and never forgive them. They always told her, not to hesitate to let them know about her fears and anxieties.

There was no place to run and hide forever, and somehow, eventually things would get better. While it was not always easy, she tried to hang on, let the bad days pass, and have the audacity to carry on.

THE BOOK GARDEN

For one who reads, there is no limit to the number of lives that may be lived, for fiction, biography, and history offer an inexhaustible number of lives in many parts of the world, in all periods of time.
—Louis L'Amour

Mari's grandfather's for life and learning new things, was contagious.

He was an avid book lover, and he encouraged her to read anything and everything. He bought her children's books, if he found good ones. One of the first English books he brought her was *Heidi*, written by Johanna Spyri, a well-known Swiss author who wrote children's stories.

The story, in a nutshell, was about the central character, Heidi, a little girl who is orphaned and goes to live with her grandfather in the Swiss alps. Heidi forms a bond with her grandfather and develops a friendship with a boy called Peter. Circumstances forced her to go Frankfurt, Germany, and work in a house for wealthy people. Heidi always longs to return to the Alps and to her grandfather and friend Peter.

Mari loved the book because she could relate to Heidi and the special bond with her grandfather and her wanting to be with him. She carried the book, until it was in tatters and worn-out, everywhere in her book bag and read it hundreds of times.

Although she read children's books and liked them, especially the series by Enid Blyton and others, she was introduced to books for adults, people at any age.

It was Grandfather setting an example again, with his personal investment in books to motivate others to develop the interest to read them. Long before book clubs were made popular by Oprah and others, he had a large collection of books and started a local book club in their home. He did not lend books, with rare exceptions.

There was a large veranda as soon as one entered the main building of the house, and it was used as a living room to entertain visitors. The aura was inclusive and welcoming for everyone to spend some time in the serene surroundings. There were large paintings in grand frames. Notably, in the center of visibility was a large replica of the painting of Jesus praying in the garden of Gethsemane.

There were also others which drew attention, replicas of two other famous oil paintings. Both paintings were gifts given to him by people who had painstakingly found and framed them.

The first one was "Sohni-Mahiwal," a painting by Sobha Singh. It was based on the folk legend story from a village in Punjab, Pakistan. The story of a woman, Sohni, who met her lover, Mahiwal, and started crossing a river with a sturdy clay pot which became a life-saving device. It was a love story but turned into a forbidden love story once Sohni married a man the family chosen for her. They continued to meet in secrecy.

During one of the secret rendezvous, the river currents grew strong, and she was afraid of drowning and called out for Mahiwal. Legend is that he swam swiftly and try to save her, although one of his legs was weak, and he had a limp. Unfortunately, both died, making it a tragic story, and making their love to seen as immortal.

The other was a replica of the great Claude Monet's painting, "The Bridge at Argenteuil." It is said that Monet created it observing people in Paris in 1874, when boating was a popular pastime. The colors are said to reflect the light on the water with a translucent effect.

There was a huge circular table made in sandalwood as the centerpiece. It was always overflowing with all the major newspapers, magazines, and some books in English and Tamil. There were bookshelves set up all around the room, with books in all genre.

The book club met once a month, to review one book. Mostly original writings in English and Tamil with occasional books which were English translations. There were about thirty invited guests from the local area from all religions and backgrounds with common literary interests, which brought and held them together. They were mostly men and a few women.

There was no membership fee, and refreshments were served with hot tea. The guest speakers took the lead, reviewed the books, and followed by a discussion with everyone for a few hours. There were agreements and disagreements, which were politely expressed. With the Captain serving as the informal facilitator for the discussions, no one would dare step out of boundaries or show disrespect to anyone.

Mari attended some of the book club meetings with the adult guests. The books reviewed were from a wide range of topics, and Grandfather made sure it did not become the same old and boring. Some book reviews were far more interesting than others and memorable.

The first book review was of the famous Tamil classic *Thirukkural* (திருக்குறள், sacred verses) written by the great Tamil poet Thiruvalluvar. It cannot be accurately dated and said to be somewhere between and the first and third-century BC. It has stood the test of time, translated into hundreds of languages with wise advice and principles to live by.

The guest speaker was a writer, well-known for his own poetry publications.

Mari knew about it since it was on the reading lists and Tamil poetry in almost all schools.

The poet reviewer recited the verses passionately. He made it more interesting and engaging. He encouraged everyone to participate, and it turned out to be a *Kurals* reciting competition, with the attendees joining in and started taking turns and reciting verses they had memorized with anecdotes.

They told stories and gave examples which exemplified Kural No. 72.

அன்பிலார் எல்லாம் தமக்குரியர்
அன்புடையார்   என்பும்   உரியர்
பிறர்க்கு. (Kural 72)

Translation:

The loveless, only belong themselves, are alone;
Those filled with love, belong to everyone.

William Shakespeare's *Macbeth* was reviewed by an English teacher, Mr. Stevens, who was a fanatic of the great Shakespeare's works. He quoted lines in dramatic fashion, and his theatrical presentation was awesome. He narrated the story very well—of the Scottish General Macbeth's political ambitions, fueled by his wife and three witches, and lead to his downfall. Later, his paranoia led to civil war, and eventually, Macbeth and his wife, Lady Macbeth, were also killed.

It was thought-provoking to Mari, and the message of the book was easily understandable to all; unbound ambitions by destroying others can lead to tragic consequences.

One of the last book reviews Mari attended was of the unique book *Rubáiyát of Omar Khayyám,* written in Persian and attributed to the astronomer-poet Omar Khayyam in the eleventh-century AD. The *Rubaiyat,* referred to as a quatrain, is a four-line form of poetry in the Persian language.

The English translation was by Edward Fitzgerald in the nineteenth century. He introduced these magnificent writings to the English-speaking world (not sure how Fitzgerald found this book). More importantly, Mari was not sure how her grandfather found this unusual book.

He liked the compilation of poems based on spiritual freedom and aspiring higher values and decided to review the book, which is appealing to the people from all faiths for its literary richness. The unusual style of original poetry with symbolism and metaphors are vivid, and he decided not to make it an analysis about religious perspectives. The sun and moon, among many others, were used as metaphor, things which were always fascinating to him.

The lines flowed with beauty and clarity.

How sad, a heart that, does not know how to love, that does not know what it is to be drunk with love. If you are not in love, how can you enjoy the blinding light of the sun, the soft light of the moon?

The book garden was in full bloom on that day, as it was on many days.

ODYSSEY

Though we travel the world over to find the beautiful,
we must carry it with us, or we find it not.
—Ralph Waldo Emerson

The magnificent silver bird with wings, with the iconic mascot Maharajah painted on the sides, was on the runway, ready to take off. Marie was ten years old, and it was her first trip alone around the globe. A new adventure for her.

Her father, Sam's wishes to travel cross the oceans to faraway lands had finally come true. He was accepted for admission in a doctoral program at New York State University in the United States of America. He was issued a student visa, and Rose received a dependent visa. They could not legally work and had to live in a one-bedroom apartment. As all immigrants, there was a process and years of difficult struggles ahead to become green-card eligible and become part of the new world.

The student financial assistance was quite limited. They could barely make it, but they always sent whatever money they could for Mari's living expenses and education. Rose knew that her father would educate Mari and take good care of her, whether they were able to send money or not, but they did their part.

Mari was doing well academically, attending good schools. They did not want to interrupt her schooling and make her leave her grandparents. Once she graduated from high school, she could decide to reunite with her parents. She was more than happy with that decision. They financially always supported Mari and sent money generously and more than needed for her schooling and other expenses. If they could not help every month for financial reasons, they compensated and caught up on payments as soon as they could.

Rose and Sam were used to living by themselves as a couple without Mari. Interestingly, just as children of parents in unhappy marriages feel conflicted, at the other extreme, are couples who are extraordinarily close to each other and have complicated relationships with their children as well.

Patty Davis, the daughter of US President Reagan and Nancy Reagan, once said in an interview,

> *If a band of gypsies came and took me and my brother Ron Reagan Jr. away, they would miss us, but they'd be fine. They would go on. Which didn't mean they didn't love us. But it meant that they were complete. They were complete unto each other. And that can be a complicated thing for children.*

It was perhaps too harsh, but she captured it aptly. The closeness of Rose and Sam as a couple was somewhat the same. It complicated their relationship with their only child.

Mari had traveled alone in buses, trains, and other automobiles, but this was her first time traveling alone in an airplane. Grandfather had prepared her for days on many levels. He told her that she was visiting her parents and time would go by, and she would be back soon. She should always respect them and try to keep them happy, especially not to have any arguments with Rose.

Mari spoke to her parents quite a few times over the phone before traveling. She felt anxious and not sure how she would get along with them. Rose was getting impatient with her repetitive questions. She once blurted out, "What is there to worry? You must be fearless. I have traveled alone many times. You will be fine. We won't let you travel if it was unsafe. We all come into this world alone and leave alone."

That was not empathetic or reassuring. But that was the way Rose spoke, direct and blunt to everyone. Whenever she would take that tough tone, Mari took a few steps back and withdrew from her mother.

Somewhere on a deeper level, she knew Rose spoke the truth. It was her way of showing tough love and offering support. We indeed come into the world alone and leave alone. It would be good to keep that in mind, learn survival skills when circumstances made it necessary to be away from the places and people who are familiar to us.

In the tradition, which her grandparents followed, before any family member traveled to faraway places, her grandmother played the old hymn, "God be with you till we meet again, 'Neath His wings protect and hide you."

Following that, Grandfather prayed for travel mercies and read the verses from Psalm 91:

> *The Lord is thy keeper: The Lord is thy shade upon thy right hand. The sun shall not smite thee by day, nor the moon by night. The LORD shall preserve thee from all evil: he shall preserve thy soul. The LORD shall preserve thy going out and thy coming in from this time forth, and even for evermore.*

That made her feel better. She was given clear instructions and was assured that everyone who was designated to assist her in the airlines, and the airports would take good care of her.

Her parents would meet her once she landed at the destination in the United States. She must be always aware and watchful of surroundings, and if anything did not feel right, tell those who could help her, and everything would be okay.

Mari had her small travel air bag and suitcase packed and ready. She wore the badge "Unaccompanied Minor" in bold letters linked to a chain around her neck. The thousands of miles across the oceans was not something she could comprehend, and it was perhaps the reason that she was unafraid of the journey itself.

A pretty woman in a purple and green *saree*, with mango designs, welcomed them into the aircraft and another dressed like her was assigned to take care of Mari. There were two other minor children traveling with her to New York. Marie's seat was close to the lady, who asked her, "Do you want some candy? Is this your first time traveling by yourself?"

Marie nodded vigorously. The woman smiled and said, "It will be okay. Call me Miss Rita and ask me if you need anything." She showed her how to fasten her seat belt, helped her and offered her some orange candy. She held on to the seat handles as the airplane started move slow. It suddenly picked up speed, rushed into the runway at high speeds, and took off.

Marie felt a little nauseous but tried to settle down. She looked around. She saw all kinds of people traveling together. They were in all age groups, dressed in all kinds of international attires. Some she had never seen before.

There were stops and transits to connecting flights. Miss Rita and all the flight attendants who were assigned to take care of her went above and beyond to make her feel comfortable. After stops and transits in New Delhi, London, New York, Mari was on the last connecting flight. Although everyone took good care of her, the long travel across time zones was extremely exhausting. "Ladies and gentlemen, fasten your seat belts. Stay in your seats. We will be landing soon in Atlanta, Georgia."

She looked outside the window; the plane was flying in low altitude. She saw the trees, greenery in the middle of brown soil; lakes, and ponds, which looked the same as in India. When the airplane wheels touched down on the ground in America, it did not make her feel nervous, like she had arrived in an unknown foreign land to her.

Mari felt like she had safely descended from the heavens to the soil below at the other end of the world which felt familiar and safe, something mysterious, which could not be explained.

The airline staff, who were her chaperones, took good care of her to the very end. They helped with the US customs and immigration procedures. The immigration officer was friendly and not intimidating. He smiled and made her relax. Grandfather had prepared her.

"Be respectful and courteous. You will meet good people there. Learn to adjust to the new land."

As she came outside to the waiting area, she saw Rose and Sam waiting for her. Rose said, "Welcome to America, Marigold." She had that naughty look when she teased people and played practical jokes.

Sam smiled and told Rose, "Don't scare the poor child."

In a reassuring voice, he said, "Mummy is being playful with you. She was waiting for you. Everything is all right." Mari felt better seeing Sam come to her defense and hoped for time with them to go by soon.

Thus began the odyssey of global travels across miles, continents, and oceans for decades to come.

*****

Mari's reminiscing was interrupted. It was the receptionist at the counseling center. "Dr. Sam, your last appointment cancelled. Can we go home early?"

"That will be fine. It gives me more time to go home and get ready for the Christmas choir concert tonight."

CAN'T HAVE EVERYTHING
WE WANT

*If you have kindness in your heart, you offer acts of kindness
to touch the hearts of others wherever you go—whether they
are random or planned. Kindness becomes a way of life.*
—Roy T. Bennett

Mari was on time. The centerstage was set for the Christmas concert in the church auditorium. The spotlight moved around brightly on the faces on stage, ready to show off their musical talents.

In the row ahead of Mari, a colleague who works with her was seated with her family. By her side was an energetic little girl who was about five or six years old. She turned around and smiled at Mari. She seemed to be bored and frequently turned around and smiled and waved at her. Mari responded and gently waved back at her.

Her parents noticed that her restlessness was becoming a distraction to everyone and tried to quiet her. "Shh...shh."

The little girl did not give up. She made an extended fixating eye contact with Mari with her twinkling eyes. She did all kinds of things to get her attention, tried to give her a hymnbook from her aisle, and said something in a whispering voice.

It was not hard to lip-read what she was saying. "What is your name?"

Her mother pulled her dress collar and made her sit still. She was quiet for a few minutes but repeated the question, "What's is your name?"

It was becoming more disruptive, so Mari looked away, avoiding all eye contact with the girl. She seemed to settle down.

At the end of the concert, she exchanged a few pleasantries with her colleague. She then leaned forward and shook hands with the girl.

"My name is Mari. What is your name?"

"Lauren," the girl replied.

*****

About a month later, Mari was working in her office when she heard a knock at her door. It was her colleague and Lauren. "Her school closed early, and she is here with me. She wanted to see you."

"Hello, Lauren!"

Lauren was shy. Lauren's mother received a call on her cell phone. "Can she stay with you for a few minutes? I have to go my office, will be right back."

"Sure, take your time."

Lauren seemed to get comfortable. She walked around Mari's office with her hands on her hips and looked at all the pictures. "Who is this? And this?" Mari told her all their names.

"Ah, so many pictures. People gave you so many pictures?"

"Yes, they do, and I put them up there." She went on tell her about some of the people in the pictures.

"Who is this boy?"

"It's my son."

Lauren paused and wondered about something. "But where is your baby girl's picture?"

"My baby girl?" Mari asked Lauren for clarification. "Who are you asking me about, Lauren?"

"Where is your baby girl? Your daughter?"

"Oh, I don't have a daughter!"

Lauren was curious and persistent. "Did you want her?"

"A daughter? Of course I did. I badly wanted her!" Mari made a sad face and said, "I really did want her."

Lauren seemed to understand and almost intuitively said, "You wanted a baby girl, but you just couldn't have her? Hmm." Lauren became animated and threw her arms up in the air.

44

It was too funny. Mari had to try to hard control herself from laughing and pretended to be serious. "I really wanted her but couldn't have her."

There was a pause. Lauren came over to Mari and put her arms around her.

"It's okay, Mari, don't be sad. My mommy says we can't have everything we want."

Mari was taken aback. Where did that come from? It was adorable and profound as she simplified dealing with disappointments, as adults struggle to do, in a sensitive and nurturing way.

Lauren then changed the topic and told Mari all about her baby brother, taking pride in the way in which she helped her mother take care of him.

*****

A few days later.

It was another late afternoon. The door was open to Mari's office, and her new friend little, Lauren, came running inside.

"Hello, Lauren, how are you?"

"I'm good, Mari. See what I brought you!"

It was a lovely picture of her in a nice picture frame. Mari was really surprised. "Wow, that is beautiful, and it is very sweet of you. Thank you so much!"

Lauren even picked a spot for the picture. "Mari, you should put my picture right next to your boy's picture."

"Sure, I will do that, wouldn't put it anywhere else!"

Mari gave Lauren a hug and followed her orders as she looked on. Lauren looked happy to see the picture placed in the spot she wanted to.

Mari was deeply moved by the unexpected kindness. She knew that in a few years, little Lauren will grow up and will forget all about her and these moments. However, she would always remember the heartwarming gesture of a kind girl who went out of her way and tried to make her feel better with her most thoughtful words and gift.

BAD THINGS HAPPEN
TO GOOD PEOPLE

Many of us have been touched by the magic
of a great teacher. I know I have.

—Bruce Rauner

Mari had some magic dust sprinkled on by a great teacher, Mrs. Ruby Jacob.

Mari was fond of her and called her Ruby Teacher; she was an amazing mentor. Her presence and personal support made all the difference in the important high school years and contributed greatly to her academic success.

Education was extremely important in her family. Her grandfather was the alumnus of Central High School. It was a private coeducational high school which was affordable. It had provided good education to him and many others who were able to go excel in various professional fields, and some went on to become national leaders. He was proud of his school and felt that it was important for his first grandchild, girl or boy, to attend and graduate as he did from the Central High School.

He wanted Mari to study all the subjects in English medium. It would be easier if she decided to attend professional colleges or medical college. He motivated her to go into the helping professions without making it openly known and placing too much pressure on her. He would often talk about Dr. Ida Scudder, a young American lady doctor, who gave up her comfortable life in the USA and moved to India to provide the much-needed quality health care for women.

There were only few girls in the English medium sections. With the onset of adolescence and puberty, most families, for cultural reasons, transferred them to all-girls schools. Mari's grandfather was confident that Mari would be fine and handle it all. With everyone in the town knowing him, and the strict reputation of his friend the headmaster, Mr. Balan Stevens; he was convinced that she would be safe and focus well.

Mari was perceived as a studious and nerdy girl, wearing thick eyeglasses. She had her own small chair and desk in the front of class all by herself while the boys sat in long benches with desks behind her. It would have been a strange situation for any girl, spending all day and studying in an all-boys classroom for three years. The years when hormones were beginning to show their manifestations with budding sexual attractions. She was expected to be a well-behaved girl, to study hard, to graduate with high scores, and to be accepted in a prestigious institution of higher learning.

She tried to be all that, but she certainly had her share of bad girl and bad student moments; like all adolescent and teenage students with plenty of challenges, problems, and distractions.

Mrs. Ruby Jacob was her social studies teacher. Her persona was calm and kind. She was among the few women teachers at the school. They developed a good student-teacher bond, someone she trusted, and would talk about her all the time at home.

Mari's grandmother, the wise woman that she was, knew that Mari really needed a woman teacher at school who could help if needed. She could advise and protect her since she was surrounded by mostly boys and men at school. She visited with Ruby Teacher privately at her home and requested that she take Mari under her wings and watch over her.

Ruby Teacher assured Mari's grandmother that she would take good care of her and not to worry. And she kept her word. She would check on Mari from time to time. Ruby Teacher was someone she could trust and talk to about almost anything. She genuinely cared, reminded her to be careful, focus on her studies, and encouraged her that everything will be okay. When Mari selected chemistry as her elective subject, she needed some extra tutoring help. Ruby Teacher suggested that her husband, Mr. Jacob, who was also a teacher at another school, could help her with tutoring.

Mari looked forward to going to Ruby Teacher's house with two other students for tuition classes. Ruby Teacher had three energetic young sons, and the youngest one was a toddler. He was adorable and looked like a boy baby model who was featured in advertisements. She played with him and had fun while learning. Mr. Jacob made the fundamentals of chemistry easy to understand and taught her with dedication.

With the encouragement of her grandparents and support from her teachers, especially Ruby Teacher and her husband, Mari graduated with the high scores in the public exams and was accepted to attend one of the best medical colleges in the country.

In less than two years, Mari heard the sad news that Ruby Teacher was diagnosed with an aggressive form of breast cancer with metastasis. Her condition deteriorated quickly, and she was terminally ill in the hospital.

Grandfather insisted that she come home as soon as possible, and they visited her in the hospital. Ruby Teacher could barely speak, had lost a lot of weight, and appeared very weak. She recognized Mari and squeezed her hand and tried to smile. It was the last time she saw Ruby Teacher, who passed away much too young. Mari always wondered about her family, Mr. Jacob and the lovely children, and how much they must have missed her and missed out in having a wonderful mother.

"Why do bad things happen to good people like Ruby Teacher?"

That eternal question has no real answers. When we are faced with the reality that loved ones who are dear to us have serious illnesses and there is the real possibility of losing them, our faith is shaken to the core, and we struggle to hold on to it.

Mari remembered the question posed by Rabbi Harold Kushner in his famous book, *When Bad Things Happen to Good People*, while dealing with this eternal question, and it ended by suggesting, "A better question would be 'Now that this has happened to me, what am I going to do about it?'"

COMFORT FROM ABOVE

The nitrogen in our DNA, the calcium in our teeth, the iron in our blood, the carbon in our apple pies were made in the interiors of collapsing stars. We are made of star stuff.
—Carl Sagan, *Cosmos*

Mari was feeling devastated. It was the first time she experienced intense loss and grief in a personal way and the void it leaves forever. She had returned to her grandparents' home from Madras, a city about two hours away, attending medical college to visit Ruby Teacher in the hospital.

Even since her childhood, when there were days with bad news and disappointments, one way her grandfather would try to comfort and encourage Mari was to take her to the garden or terrace to look at the night skies. They would look at the beautiful moon and the constellations of the stars.

Grandfather would tell her about the wonders of the sky with historical anecdotes. He was a good storyteller and would include stories from different ancient cultures and how the explorers of the space viewed them. He was particularly fascinated by Orion, the Hunter, which was a band of three bright stars. The Orion was identified thousands of years ago and was known as the hunter, shepherd, and warrior.

It is no wonder that the stars and heavens have been forever the significant and notable subject of the arts, literature, and religious writings. Blue, orange, purple, or gray skies, if not for the stars and stargazers, there would not be spectacular sky explorations.

Even if one is skeptical about their mystical powers from above, as those who studied astronomy believe, even scientists in the fields

49

of aeronautics and astroscience find the skies endlessly fascinating and space explorations continue.

As soon as Mari calmed down and was temporarily distracted from her worries, engrossed looking at the skies above, Grandfather would remind her to keep things in perspective. "Everything is relative," he would say, "we humans are tiny creatures living on a planet called Earth, looking into the vast universe. While it was hard to experience disappointments, it was not, literally, the end of the world."

The Sun would come up and shine the next day and the Moon the next night, life would go on.

It always made Mari feel a little better, to ponder about the vastness of the universe and our places within it with a mix of hope and reverence.

"Look there, Marima," Grandfather pointed to a bright, twinkling star. "Ruby Teacher's light energy must have been added, to make that star extra bright. She may be around in spirit, shining above."

Mari took a deep breath, taking it all in, felt the heartache, sighed, and exhaled.

AFTER LIFE

In order to experience everyday spirituality, we need to remember that we are spiritual beings spending some time in a human body.
—Barbara De Angelis

Mari returned to her medical college.

The grief, following the death of Ruby Teacher, lingered on and made her reflect more and more about the interconnections between the physical human body, mind and soul.

The courses and practical lab studies were becoming harder, diving into the depths of human anatomy, physiology, and biochemistry.

After the introductory anatomy classes in the second year, the time came for studying the practical aspects of the human body with hands-on study. The anatomy classes were taught in a large building. The bricks painted in all red and was known as the "Red Fort."

As Mari entered the large hall with much anticipation, the stench of formalin was pungent and repulsive. She was ready for the classes but was not really prepared to see what she saw for the first time, human cadavers; dead and preserved brown human bodies on top of each other in the huge cement tanks.

As she sat down with a group of classmates in the designated table, the assistant to the anatomy professor pulled a body from the cement tank and placed it on the table. It was a female; she was a female.

She could not take her eyes off her. Darkened by the formalin and preservative solutions, the layers of the skin were toughened and had a rubbery exterior appearance. Hundreds of nerves were hanging. It looked like brown wires in different sizes, thin to thick. From inside, the reddish-brown color muscles and tissues were still connected to solid bones in her skeletal structure.

Mari pondered, *Was she really a living person not too long ago? Who was she? Was she beautiful? Was she special to someone? Anyone? What kind of life did she have, only to end up on a cold table with medical students ready to take her apart in the process of practical learning, with guides and textbooks, including the well-known Grey's Anatomy?*

It did not appear to be one of those voluntary donations of one's body to the study of science. The cadavers came from one of the largest public mortuaries in the government hospital, where unclaimed bodies were kept.

Her body, in name of the study of science, was about to be mangled and pieced. Mari wanted to show her some respect, the least she could do was to give her a name. The first name which came to mind was Cleopatra. Mari did not tell anyone that she was utterly fascinated by her. She named her Cleopatra.

She did not tell anyone. They will not understand and think she was strange. She realized that she must have inherited some strange traits from Rose and smiled to herself.

Most daughters think that they will never ever be like their mothers, inherit or display certain qualities they disliked, but inevitably, those pieces show themselves at unexpected times.

In a strange way, she looked for Cleopatra when she entered the Red Fort as parts of her slowly went missing.

The more profound questions about her began to creep into her mind. The physical body of a woman made of dead organs, tissues, and cells were displayed in front of her. What happened to her soul? Did it ever exist, and if so, was she around in spirit or forever gone missing?

More importantly, some curiosity about her own life began to emerge. Where, when, and how will her own story end? Will it be in a hospital, home, or somewhere unexpected?

Could this be me? Would I end up not in the normal way, with a funeral service, taken to a cemetery, and given a solemn burial or a graveyard to be cremated?

What if I end up as a cadaver like Cleopatra, displayed like this, with the physical body form cut into pieces in front of strangers, future doctors, forensic specialist, or anyone?

She knew to never to say never. It can never happen to her.

But for heavenly grace and mercy, it could happen to anyone.

UNBURDENING

The most beautiful people we have known are those who have known defeat, known suffering, known struggle, known loss, and have found their way out of the depths. These persons have an appreciation, a sensitivity, and an understanding of life that fills them with compassion, gentleness, and a deep loving concern. Beautiful people do not just happen.
—Elisabeth Kübler-Ross

Dr. Mari Sam's next client was waiting for her.

It was someone new, and she looked at the basic intake information on her computer screen. Mrs. Roberta Thomas was in her forties, and the reason for her visit was documented as grief counseling.

As Roberta entered her room, Mari was struck by her attractive and dignified appearance. The dark navy-blue dress with white buttons made her look elegant too.

"Hello, Ms. Thomas."

"Hello, Dr. Sam."

"Nice to meet you. Can you tell me a little about yourself, and why you are here?"

Her posture changed, and the sadness in her eyes and dark circles around them were becoming visible.

"My son was killed two weeks ago in a robbery. I have been going through a lot. We buried Bryan last week."

"I am so sorry, Ms. Thomas."

She continued, "He was only eighteen years old. His father and I dropped him off at the university only a month ago. It is unbearable to think he is gone, and I won't see him again."

Mari softly said, "It must be such a difficult time for you and your family."

She continued, "He was my baby, would not leave my side. We were so close. He would say Mama, Mama, a hundred times a day. I hear his voice every single minute of the day in my head. My family said I needed to professionally talk to someone."

After a moment of silence, she slowly gathered herself and asked Mari, "Do you have any children?"

Mari replied, "Yes, I have one son."

"So you can understand how terrible it can be to lose a child."

"It is so hard to even imagine that."

"It is all so senseless. Bryan would have given him his wallet if he wanted some money. He always helped people. Why did he have to shoot him? We told him to be careful. Sometimes, it is just being in the wrong place at the wrong time."

It was heartbreaking to see the devastation, and her pain is palpable.

She spoke about Bryan and as she did, she was going through different emotions. For a few minutes, she seemed to have some flashes of good memories, and her expression changed when she thought about how much she was looking forward to seeing him during Christmas time.

"Bryan always bought me handbags as gifts for Christmas. Mama, I will buy you that black and brown Michael Kors handbag you wanted. I told you I will buy it for you this Christmas."

She continued to talk about how they went shopping together, and he would observe the things she liked, buy them, and surprise her with them. Her tone became somber when she talked about his dreams about going to college and playing football while pursuing a career in engineering.

"Now, I have to go through this nightmare of the trial. Nothing is the same."

Mari listened for the most part, let her unburden the pent-up emotions freely and acknowledging them.

Mrs. Thomas suddenly paused and said something extraordinary.

"I feel bad for the mother of the young man who shot my son. He is also eighteen, and it must be hard for her too. I can't understand why this happened. We try to raise our children as best we can but so many things can go wrong and go wrong, and we mothers suffer like this losing our children. This is too much. I don't want anybody to go through what I am going through."

Her empathy for that other mother was touching. Mari was deeply moved and became speechless.

She may be in shock and pain but the unmistakable goodness in her comes through.

"You are an amazing lady," Mari said softly.

"I don't know about that. I can't talk to my family about everything. They are devastated and going through a lot. I am afraid for them and how they can handle all this."

It was obvious who the "central rock" of that family was; a lady of grace and strength trying to hold the family together—and not let it fall apart.

People who are the rocks in the family need safe places to unburden too.

The session lasted longer than scheduled.

As Mrs. Thomas left, she said, "I think this is helping me. Can I see you again soon?"

Mari replied, "Of course, we can meet in two weeks. You can call me if you want to come in before that."

FOR A REASON
AND SEASON

Love is like the wild rose-briar,
Friendship like the holly-tree.
The holly is dark when the rose-briar blooms
But which will bloom most constantly?
                              —Emily Bronte, *Love and Friendship*

The seasons began to change with the monsoon and rains arriving, and there were major transitions to come.

Mari was in the final year of medical college, and it was a hectic period for her, studying and completing clinical rotations in various hospitals. She could not visit her grandparents as often as she could. They had a house in the city of Madras, where she was studying, and they stayed mostly there to be closer to her during the critical and stressful years before her graduation.

Even as the transitions were going on, some things never changed, like their kindness and warm hospitality to everyone. Mari would take her friends from college to visit them. Her close friend Mala would frequently accompany her. Her grandparents liked Mala, who was smart and charming.

Mala's family was among the hundreds of refugees from Burma (now called Myanmar). The refugees had roots in Tamil Nadu and returned in the 1940s and '50s after the invasion of Japan.

They had worked hard and lived affluent lives in Burma but had to leave everything behind as refugees do. Mala's family, as refugees, had major economic struggles in India and lived in a small apartment, working menial jobs. Mari's grandparents gave credit to

Mala's academic achievements and ambitions and the long way she had come to becoming a doctor. They offered her encouragement to be successful.

Mala was the oldest child in her family, and every one of them had made personal sacrifices to support her. Her parents, in fact, had stopped some of her younger siblings from going to college, and sent them to work, to support Mala financially. They had huge expectations for her after her graduation and could not wait for her to start working.

The public general hospitals where Mari worked, as she was completing her clinicals, were among largest in the country, with thousands of patients being treated every day. It was an awesome sight to see the crowds and how the hospitals could accommodate all the patients from around the State and other States without turning them away.

Grandfather stopped by to see Mari from time to time. He was happy and full of pride seeing her in her white coat, stethoscope around her neck, and working hard to become a part of the noble profession—helping to alleviate suffering and save lives. She would tell him about all the interesting and usual cases, and he would listen closely with much interest.

Mari and Mala were assigned to different hospitals, and since their schedules were hectic, they had not seen each other for some time. Late one evening, Mala came to see Mari in the hospital living quarters. She looked different and had gained some weight. Mari did not comment on it.

Mala said, "I have something important to tell you."

She continued, "I am in love with someone and pregnant."

Mari was totally surprised as Mala continued, "I think I am only two or three months pregnant, and I want to terminate this pregnancy."

Mari snapped, "What do you mean by two or three months? You don't you know for sure. Didn't you go for a checkup?"

Mala replied, "I am scared. I have not told anyone, and I don't know what to do. Can you come tomorrow with me to a private OB clinic?" Mari agreed.

The next day, they went to the private clinic, and the ultrasound showed that she was twenty-two weeks pregnant, well into her second trimester. Mala started crying. "I can't have the abortion. What I am going to do now?"

She had hidden her pregnancy from everyone. Her large white coat helped to cover up her abdomen.

There were only eight months left before taking the final exams to graduate in the final year. There was incredible pressure on everyone, and there was much at stake about the future.

Mari said, "Well, you have to tell your mother now. She may be upset, but she will understand. I will come with you." Mari had been to their home a few times, and her mother was always cordial to her.

They went together to Mala's home where her mother was alone by herself. As soon as she saw them, she intuitively knew why they had come together.

She was livid and yelled at Mala, "I knew you were pregnant. I had five children including you, don't you think I noticed? I waited for you to tell me, and you brought your friend. How could you become pregnant before marriage? How I can tell your father? He could not bear it. How can we face people and society? You have ruined all our lives. Your father and I have no choice but to die now in shame. Our hopes are dashed. Our lives have ended."

Mari tried to say something to Mala's mother, who angrily screamed, hitting her chest with her hands. "Take your friend with you until she gets rid of the thing she is pregnant with. I don't care what you do. Get rid of it, kill it if you must. Once it is gone, bring her back. We gave our lives for her to be educated. I want only my daughter back." She went inside and locked herself in a room.

It was shocking to Mari. She did not expect such a dramatic response. Mala went and banged on the door of the room her mother was in, crying, begging, and pleading to forgive her. Her mother kept telling her to go away.

Mala said, "I told you. No one in my family, or anyone for that matter, will understand. I was such a fool. What do we do now? Where can I go?"

"What about the man you are in love with? Can't you ask him to help you?" Mari had not met him. Mala had kept everything secretive from Mari, her close friend too.

She replied, "He is much younger than me, is a college student, and stays with his parents. He does not have money of his own. We are from different castes, and they are rich. They will not accept us getting married. Once I told him that I was pregnant, he has been afraid, distancing himself and avoiding me. I don't know what to do. Can you help me?"

Mari wanted to be angry and scold her, but it was too late. She desperately needed help. They talked about the one possible option available. Mari was firm and wanted assurances from Mala, about what needs to happen for that option. Then, she felt sorry for her and told her to be strong. She thought of the only place she could go for help, so she told Mala to come back to see her the next day.

As she always did during times of need, Mari went to see her grandparents that night. It was awkward to talk about the situation and trouble Mala was in, but there was no choice.

"Grandpa and Amma, can you help Mala? Can she stay for a few months with you until she has the baby? She has no place to go. If she can have the baby and complete the final exams, that will be so helpful."

They were calm, did not say anything judgmental about Mala, or how foolish she was and blame her, as most elders would have understandably under the cultural conditions and circumstances.

Nesa said, "It is a huge responsibility for us, Marima. What if her parents or the baby's father create problems for us? What is she going to do after the baby is born?"

Mari said, "I have talked to her. She has promised me that the baby's father and her family will not come to visit and cause any problems. She will be low-key. I will also make sure that she keeps her promise. She wants to give the baby up for adoption."

Grandfather looked at Nesa and said, as only he would, "She can come and stay with us until the baby is born and continue to go to college as long as she can before the baby's birth." Nesa and Mari were not surprised, knowing Grandfather, the human form of refuge.

Mari had tears in her eyes and was greatly moved by their kindness and willingness to help her friend without judgment or any expectations in return. There was absolutely no benefit in this for them, only risks and unnecessary responsibilities. They were also getting older, not young anymore. Mari could not thank them enough.

For the next three months, Mala stayed with them. Mari's amazing angelic grandparents created a nice space with privacy for her to live and study. They provided the most loving care, with nutritional foods and everything a pregnant woman needed.

Mala's father came to see her only once for a brief visit. No one else from her family came to see her. He brought some fruits and Indian sweets and thanked Mari's grandparents for taking care of her. There was not much conversation, and he did not ask about the financial and other expenses for her care or her imminent delivery or her return to their home.

Surprisingly, when Rose and Sam knew about what was going on, they were supportive and volunteered to pay for Mala's prenatal and delivery expenses.

Since Mala wanted to proceed with the adoption of the baby, Grandfather had contacted an attorney who dealt with legal adoptions and families who wanted to adopt children. Mala spoke to him a few times and gave her voluntary consent for the process to be in place.

On a full moon night, Mala gave birth to a beautiful baby girl, with Mari by her side. It was a normal vaginal delivery with no complications.

The next day, she came back to the home of Mari's grandparents, where the adoption was to take place. Mala was not a Christian but wanted the baby to have a Christian name. Mari named her Sarah Sangeeta. Sarah was from the Bible. In Hebrew, it meant *princess,* and *Sangeeta* in Tamil meant *music.* Grandfather said a short prayer and blessed the baby. The attorney was there with the adoption papers to be signed, with a representative from the adoptive family. Mala did not show publicly show any emotions as she gave the baby to Mari, to be given to the family representative. There were no dramatic moments. It happened quickly. Mala stayed for two more days with them and went back to her parents' home.

A few weeks later, Mala returned to classes at their college. She seemed all right, and Mari asked her if she was all right, and no other questions were asked about what happened when she went home or with the father of the baby.

They avoided talking about what had happened during those months. They carried on as usual, as if it never happened. Mari and Mala graduated from medical college on time and as scheduled.

*****

Their friendship may have been meant for a season, as Mala began to drift away. Mari was also busy getting ready to get married and move to America.

The roots of love will always remain in some friendships and relationships, while the branches grow distant in different directions.

LIFE MARKERS

*What we once enjoyed and deeply loved we can never
lose, for all that we love deeply becomes part of us.*
                                                    —Helen Keller

The years went by.

Although it may seem slow and stuck at times, precious time with the people we love and care about goes by real fast.

After receiving her medical degree, Mari married the man love she loved, and they decided to move to America. She wanted to specialize and serve as a mental health specialist, a psychiatrist or psychologist. It was not to "fix" people but rather, be there for them in a professional capacity, to help find the courage and audacity to survive and carry on. With the twists and turns in her career path, she became a licensed clinical psychologist.

Everyone has life markers, significant events in their lives marked deeply in their heart and brain. They are life markers where life can be separated into different parts, before and after that event. They are often difficult, traumatic, and inevitable.

Saying goodbye to her grandparents and parting with them at the Madras airport was one of the most unbearable, gut-wrenching life markers in Mari's life. She felt like the deep connections to her vital organs were being severed.

Captain, the old warrior that he was, controlled the tears filled in his eyes. Mari and her grandmother, Nesa, cried, sobbing and wailing. She slowly walked away from them after hugging and kissing them. When she turned around, she saw her grandfather slowly walking backward and waving his handkerchief. It was agonizing to see his soldier's swagger so diminished. He was almost stumbling, trying not to fall.

She heard him say loudly, "Marima, the living God be with you. We love you and will be waiting for you, until we meet again."

That would be the last time she would see her grandparents.

******

Rose and Sam, after having lived the United States for thirty years, made the decision to move back to India after their retirement. It was not an easy decision, but they had missed big parts of life in India, with their siblings and close relatives. It was also Sam's wish for his final resting place, and that would be in Indian soil next to their loved ones.

They promised to visit Mari and her family every year. Life does not often unfold into our planned dream lives with happy endings. Sam had a massive heart attack and died a few weeks before his first visit back to the United States.

HOMECOMING YEARS

Kindness is universal. Sometimes being kind allows others to see the goodness in humanity through you. Always be kinder than necessary.
—Germany Kent

Rose lived alone for years in the nice home, in India, she and Sam had built together. Although she had moved back to her homeland, America was dear to her and had a special place of love embedded in her heart.

All immigrants can relate to living conflicted lives forever. Loving two countries deeply at the same time without comparisons and measurements, which are not necessary to make one feel better than the other. Since one can live in only one place at a time, it does not stop the heart from continuing to wander back and forth between the two lands.

For a woman with wanderlust, Rose shared her heart between India and America. She would become passionate and fiercely defend the United States if anyone said anything even remotely negative about the United States and try to make them regret what they said.

A relative once told Mari about an incident, where he witnessed Rose traveling in an electric train compartment with him. The people traveling with them were total strangers.

A group of men, who seemed educated, had a newspaper and discussing world affairs. As the topic turned to discussing America, they said something unkind and laughed about it. Rose could hear it, and she waited but could not bear it anymore. She literally went up to the men and made a scene and stated how she lived in the United States for more than three decades, and even with the problems, it was an awesome country. She listed the reasons for its greatness with a lesson in history. They were shocked and speechless, and at the end of it, they gave her a standing ovation. It would have perhaps gone viral, if cell phones were around at that time.

She also strongly felt that since Americans were kind and embraced her as stranger, she should try to do the same. If she came across Americans who were visiting or staying in India, she would reach out to them and extend hospitality as much as she could.

One day, when she was at a restaurant, she saw a large group of young people with an elderly man. "Hello, are you Americans?"

The elderly man replied, "Yes, I am Professor Boyd, and I teach religion in a College in Michigan. These are my students. I take them around the world to different countries to see and learn about various religions and see how they are practiced in various cultural traditions for themselves. I make sure India is on the list of countries to visit, for them to have their own rich experiences."

Rose was thrilled. "I lived in the United States for more than years. Please come and bring your students to my home for dinner tomorrow." The next day, they visited Rose, and she entertained them with an elaborate dinner. She had invited a few of her Indian friends and relatives to show off her "American friends."

She was an excellent storyteller and told them about the history of India and how religions were practiced from centuries ago to contemporary times in detail. She also included a small testimony of her own Christian faith and how she leaned on her faith as a whether she was part of the religious minority or majority in both countries throughout her life.

They were captivated by her, the stories, and her great hospitality. Dr. Boyd was quite pleased. When they returned to the US and the students were asked to write essays about their global trip, all of them remembered Rose and how memorable she made the trip to India. One student wrote, "Rose was the best person we met during the entire trip, and we learned so much from her, in some ways she embodies everything India is about to me."

For the next thirteen years, Dr. Boyd included a stop at Rose's house in all his annual international trips and made sure that his students visited her. Rose felt glad that she was able to entertain them. Some small way of giving back to the wonderful Americans who had helped her over the years.

She usually gave them a souvenir, something handmade in the local community, and a scented candle when she said goodbye to them. "Share the light wherever you may go."

CHANCES AND DANCES

Looking back on the memory of, the dance
we shared 'neath the stars above
For a moment all the world was right, how could
I have known that you'd ever say goodbye
And now I'm glad, I didn't know, the way it
all would end, the way it would go
Our lives are better left to chance, I could have missed the pain,
But I'd have had to miss the dance.

—Tony Arata
(Garth Brooks—"The Dance")

The international travel was becoming more tedious and stressful for Rose, and it's taking a toll with the other health issues. She tried to always remain physically active, but the yearly travel to America, to see Mari and her family, was becoming more difficult. She did not travel every year, and Mari started visiting her in India every year.

Because of her work schedules, her visits were usually for a week. They tried to make the most of the time they spent together time. As soon as Mari arrived in India, although she was exhausted after almost thirty hours of travel, her first visit was to the cemetery to pay respect to her loved ones. The cemetery was not too far from the home of Rose. After leaving her travel luggage and some freshening up, they went together.

If the flight arrived at midnight, they hardly slept, spent time talking, and they would go first thing in the morning. They would go by an auto-rickshaw or cab and buy some flower garlands on the way to place on the graves of their loved ones. Mari would also go to the cemetery, one more time by herself, before she returned to America.

On one such mornings, they had called the cab, the driver was there waiting for them. Rose had left something behind, and she went inside the home to get it.

As Mari was sitting alone and waiting in the cab, the driver asked her, "Ma'am, are you her daughter from America?"

Mari said, "Yes."

He smiled and said, "You have an unusual mother. She is different from anyone I have ever met in my life."

He went on, "She is a very bold woman, not afraid of anything or anyone. If she is so strong and independent at this age and won't listen to anyone, I can only imagine how she must have been when she was younger! She must have been a handful to handle for your father and you. No one could have tamed her. She is a wild tigress!"

Mari smiled and listened.

His voice turned tender. "But you know, there is also has a saintly side to her. She helps a lot of people who come to her, buy foods and other things and asks me to take her to people who live far away. It may be homeless people on the street or families waiting outside in hospital grounds who are random strangers, she does not usually know. It may be to the homes where the elderly lived alone, different places, and she does it all alone and all the time. She does it quietly, without anyone knowing. She would tell me and the other cabdrivers not to tell anyone too. She is different. You can't find extraordinary people like her. You don't have to worry. That is why people will not harm her. They are respectfully afraid of her. As we say, it still rains on this bad earth because of few people like her. Otherwise, the world would be dry land without rains, and people are selfish and only care about themselves and their families. No one cares about others."

Rose had done it again. She had triggered all kinds of mixed emotions in everyone who encountered her. She was indeed a complex person, with many shades and dimensions and how she was perceived. She was all in the eyes of the beholder. To listen to a stranger who had observed her mother so closely and capture her entire nature and express his perceptions was fascinating and heartwarming.

When they arrived at the gates of the cemetery, Mari looked up at the hill close to it and saw St. Thomas Mount Church built on top of it. It was built it in the sixteenth century and said to be one of the places where St. Thomas, an apostle of Jesus, visited when he came to India. His remains in another basilica, in the same city of Madras, was built to entomb them.

Rose and Mari walked to the area where all their loved ones were laid to rest. A gentle breeze began to blow. The graves of Captain, Nesa, and Sam were all in a row, next to each other, with hibiscus and rose plants planted all around. There was a small vacant plot of land at the end. Rose pointed to it and said, "That plot of land is reserved for me. It has a nice view of the hill, and I can rest in peace."

Mari was placing flower garlands they had brought with them. She heard what Rose said and did not make a big deal and try to feign sad emotions. Rose placed small bouquets of pink and white roses on all of them. They spent some time in the cemetery, also placing flowers on graves of other extended family members and friends.

At a distance, there was an older man alone, placing Samandhi-yellow chrysanthemum flowers on a grave. He had a few red heart shaped balloons which had happy birthday and love written on them. He was a stranger, but Rose wanted to talk to him, so they walked over to where he was.

"Is it your wife's birthday? The Samandhi flowers are lovely."

"Yes, it had been twenty years since she has been gone. I miss her. Life has never been the same without her. Samandhi flowers were her favorite."

He went on and told them about how they celebrated her birthdays every year in a grand manner. They were reunions, with relatives and friends near and far away would come, and they would have grand celebrations. He looked sad when he said that no one remembers it, even his children don't remember their mother's birthday anymore.

Rose said, "I know. My loved ones are gone, but the love never dies. We have to carry on until we meet them again in heaven. You take care of yourself and your health."

He appeared to be moved and gave Rose and Mari some strands of Samandhi flowers, which he had in a bag and not placed on the grave.

Rose thought for a minute and invited the gentleman, "Would you like to come and have lunch with us at a restaurant? What is your wife's name?"

He replied, "Her name was Sheila."

"Oh, we will celebrate Sheila's birthday."

He was pleasantly surprised and agreed to come with them. He was a retired engineer, and during their conversation, they soon discovered that they had distant connections and common friends. May be there are only six degrees of separation between us all on this planet.

After a delicious lunch, Rose ordered some special desserts to celebrate Sheila's birthday.

She smiled and asked, "Marima, do you want rose milk? It has been a long time!"

"Yes, I do," Mari quickly replied. Mother and daughter drank rose milk and laughed together.

The gentleman seemed to enjoy the celebration and asked for Rose's contact information and said, "You must visit me. I will invite you soon."

And added, "I was feeling sad today. But I feel blessed meeting you. God can bring new beginnings after endings at the most unexpected times and places, even a cemetery."

WE LOVE ONLY AS
WE KNOW HOW

Love is like the sea. It's a moving thing, but still and all, it takes its shape from the shore it meets, and it's different with every shore.
— Zora Neale Hurston,
Their Eyes Were Watching God

On a hot June afternoon, Rose wanted to go to the beach with Mari. They went to Marina Beach and sat on the warm sands, watching the blue waves of the Bay of Bengal.

There was a woman with her small child selling the chickpeas snack, *sundal*. It is amazing to see how mothers can maneuver so well, around with children in their arms, back, or with them; without skipping a beat while multitasking for survival. Rose liked *sundal* and bought some *sundal*, and they sat on the sand for some time, not saying much.

After some time, they removed their sandals. They were bare feet, wanting to soak them in the water. They went slowly into the edges of the white frothy tides of the water, as they were flowing and retreating. The soft and soggy sand felt different in its feel from muddy soil. Mari felt a different kind of earthy and therapeutic connect and comfort in its own way, which made her feel relaxed.

When they returned to sit on the sands again, Rose said, "Sam would have loved this, watching the waves. I miss your dad," she paused and said, "I miss you very much."

It was the first time she was so direct. Mari did not know what to say.

Rose went on, "I always missed you but did not want to get close to you. I'm not a nurturing and sacrificing mother. I can be selfish and don't need anyone. I wanted to do whatever I wanted to and could disappear for days if I wanted to. My parents were wonderful and knew how to love you more than anyone. So I knew they will give you stability, security, and raise you well."

She sounded like biological mother talking about giving up her child for adoption, but this was a different family arrangement. She popped in and out of Mari's life, creating instability and highly interruptive at times.

"Your dad understood me as much as anyone could. I took and consumed all of him, all the spaces in his heart, and life. There was nothing much left for anyone else, even you. If he had the chance, he would been a good and caring father to you. My father was larger than life. Sam felt inadequate, and he could not compete with him for your affection."

Mari was quietly listening without any questions for some time. She was right and almost felt bad for her father Sam. It was true that Grandfather was her hero and a superman to her. No man could compete with him for her unconditional trust and respect.

She continued, "I wanted to tell you something. I am getting older, and we must talk about some important things. If you suddenly get the news that I am gone, don't feel bad about not being here with me."

It was as if she was reminding herself and me about the inevitable. "You are healthy now. Why do you want to talk about sad things and death now, Mummy?"

"Because I am almost done, almost there."

"There? Where, Mummy?" Rose smiled and point to herself and then to the sky. For someone who was always covered by a tough veneer, not letting anyone get close to her, it was raw and rare, letting her guard down and let Mari see her vulnerabilities.

She went on, "I have a few wishes. Please do not keep my body in an ice box for days until you come here. Go on with the burial quickly. Make sure I am dressed in my favorite color, in a rose-pink saree. Cynthia, your friend who helps me, will take care of everything. You can come when you can, without any pressure to take off from work. I don't care in the least about a memorial service or eulogies. Have a simple and private memorial service, if you really want to. People should say and do nice things and come and visit me when I am still around. Oh, I want you to give away packets of good food to people who not always included by society and left destitute. Do it always, here and wherever you are, and as often as you can."

She continued, "Don't worry about what people say. Don't let anyone make you feel guilty about anything. Always be brave and strong. Make yourself happy, not wait for anyone to do it for you. The world will find fault in everything, even funerals. You make all the decisions. Don't be burdened by anything with sentimentality."

She continued, "I know you want to stay close to your husband and son and will not return to India to live as we did. If you and your son don't want to live in Marigold, make good decisions. It is a special place, something which will honor God. Be worthy of your loved ones."

Mari felt a thousand different emotions, like the child she was with Rose. Always unpredictable, always complex, and unshackled love. Her mother was making it easier. Freeing her from the conflicting emotions, especially the guilt immigrants feel while dealing with aging loved ones back in their homelands.

The mother who was complicated, who she struggled to understand, and who kept the beautiful and fragrant parts of her hidden, most of the time, simplifying end of life decisions.

She was emotional and asked, "Mummy, do want me to do anything else for you now? You know I will be here if you need me."

And she asked the question that she always wondered about and weighed on her mind. "Did you ever have any regrets about having me?"

Rose reached out her hand and said, "*Kannamma*, you are my cherubim. Come and sit close to me. How could I ever regret anything that made you, anything about you? I love you more than you know."

Mari moved closer to her and held her hands. "It's all right, Mummy. I love you too."

Rose kissed Mari's hand and said, "I loved you as I know how. I wish I could have done it better. We love people in ways we only know how."

ALMOST DONE,
ALMOST THERE

There is no real ending. It's just the place where you stop the story.
—Frank Herbert

Mari gently touched the black marble plate embedded in the pillar at the entrance of the majestic home. "Marigold" was the name written in bold, golden-yellow letters on it, the dream home of Sam and Rose.

It was rebuilt brick by brick based on their dreams as they toiled, made sacrifices, and diligently saved for years. They waited patiently until they could return to India after their retirement and complete the construction. It took a long time, unlike the creation of their human offspring, Marigold, and it was left behind to take over.

Mari's heart was full of memories as she returned to the grand house, which stood strong but empty without the lives who built and guarded it for years. There had been many events—birthdays, weddings, home goings, and other celebrations.

It was about three weeks after the last and most powerful life force in that house, Rose, was gone. There was a painful silence inside the walls. The absence of her lively and boisterous presence was deeply felt.

What is an empty house without those who make it a home? The loss and absence of the warmth, caring, and yearning for you to return takes away the feelings of wanting to be there.

Sorrow began to seep into Mari's core, her being, and it began to affect her more than she ever imagined.

The relationship between a mother and daughter can often be the most complex of all family relationships. It was the same for Rose and Mari, a lifetime of conflicting emotions, volatile and tumultuous at times. But there was no denying the underlying, abiding love of two souls bonded by biology and much more.

Rose was not an ideal nurturing mother in any sense, even if such a thing exists. She never pretended to be one, yet there was something deep, fierce and loyal about her love.

How does one deal with grief? While Kubler Ross may have neatly categorized them in stages of loss and grief, in real life, it is far messier with a huge void nothing or no one can fill.

It was Mari's responsibility, as their only child, to complete the final formalities and bringing the chapter of life in Marigold the house to an end. She was a technically an orphan, severed psychologically from the umbilical cord bond.

Rose had lived a minimalist lifestyle and given away much of the valuable material things. It was her nature not to hoard or keep much and give away things on a regular basis, replacing only those which were needed. Some of the basic furniture and appliances remained.

Mari did not have siblings or siblings of Rose and Sam to fight over anything they owned. The process did not include the stress of fighting over the most insignificant things after a loved one's death, in the name of sentimentality and such. It was easy to give away what remained without any feelings.

In the end, Rose was her father's daughter, the captain's daughter. Time had mellowed her, and she was more like him in the final years of her life. She also liked to read and write and had a collection of eclectic books. And her organizational skills were meticulous.

Everything important, especially papers related to her financial and legal matters, were neatly arranged in folders and labeled to make it easier for Mari. She was thoughtful and practical in that regard. On a certain level, *thoughtful and practical,* could be two words which can be aptly used to describe the way Rose handled all matters, even as she approached the end-of-life happenings.

She knew that Mari may not be able to come right away from America if the inevitable suddenly happened to her. She had accepted that reality and expressed her wishes to Mari about the final arrange-ments for her journey and emphasized that there should be no guilt or sorrow about not being there.

There was a plaque made in rosewood, painted with the words, "Born into this world alone, we leave alone," on the wall in her bed-room. It was among her frequent sayings, and someone must have beautifully handcrafted it for her. There was a picture of a bouquet of pink roses with the quote, "Love understands, and therefore waits." And a wooden cross on the television stand. She must have found inner strength, looking at them when she was alone, and her spirit was low.

In the corner of the nightstand next to her bed was Rose's old Bible and a picture album. Mari picked up the album and opened it, and a few pictures and cards fell out of it. They were mostly of Sam, Mari, and her parents, handwritten cards and letters from them. She looked at them for some time.

The Bible looks marred. She must have used it all the time, and she had written a lot of notes and references all over it. There are many underlined scriptural verses in red ink. The bookmark she had used had dry rose flower petals stuck to them with a bird feather and had the following Bible verse:

> *A new command I give you: Love one another. As I have loved you, so you must love one another. By this everyone will know that you are my disci-ples, if you love one another.* (John 13:34–35 New International Version)

There were acronyms that looked like codes for something. Mari could not really figure them out. Her calligraphic handwriting had a way of enhancing her written words, even aging did not change it.

Mari took the Bible and the album, the treasures that they were, with legacies and lifetimes captured inside them. She removed the plaque, picture, and cross and carefully packed them, to take them with her.

The skies were getting dark with clouds, about to open and put on a glorious show of a hailstorm. There were silver lightning strikes and roaring thunder.

Lines from Rose's favorite song emerged from her memory bank:

> I hear the mighty thunder, thy power
> throughout the universe displayed;
> Then sings my soul, my Savior God to thee,
> how great thou art, how great thou art!

She heard the voice of the cabdriver say, "*Akka*, there is a bad hailstorm coming. We have to leave."

Mari replied, "I am almost done. I am almost there."

She took it all in and inhaled and looked up to the skies as she exhaled.

Sometimes just to say your own truth loud
is enough to find others like you.
—Matt Haig, *The Midnight Library*

WE CARRY ON

If you are feeling lonely and lost
As your eyes meet my words
On the page of the book you hold
On glass screens on some device
This was meant to be
You connecting with me

Are you feeling the life fatigue
That gaping void and ennui
From all the sudden changes
In the slow and stuck life cycles
Your sparkle subdued
With postponed dreams

Does it dull your shine
When you think about your existence
And wonder about the grand purpose
With no real answers
Lost and drowning
Looking for a spark

Know you are not alone, never alone
With a glowing spirit inside, vibrant life outside
You matter, have every right live
Don't you give up, for I too am trying
Not knowing what comes next
Living and loving as I know how

(June Samuel)

GLOSSARY

akka. Tamil word to mean an older sister or an older-sister figure.

appam. Word in the Tamil language. Soft hoppers made from a mix of fermented rice and coconut batter.

auto-rickshaw. Motorized vehicle with three wheels. It is a common form of urban transport in many countries around the world.

biryani. Indian dish made with seasoning of rice with many spices and meat, fish, or vegetables.

curry. Indian-style, spiced gravy dish with onions and tomatoes; meats and vegetables are added.

golusu. A word in the Tamil language meaning anklets with Indian jewelry designs.

kannamma. A word in Tamil referring to the one precious like the eyes.

samandhi. A word in the Tamil language. A variety of chrysanthemum flowers, golden yellow in color.

sundal. A word in the Tamil language. It refers to a snack made with legumes, such as chickpeas and peanuts with coconut flakes.

Tamil language. Among the longest surviving classical languages, with history dating back to 300 BC. Today, globally, more than seventy million speak the language.

vadai. A word in the Tamil language. A deep-fried snack, generally made with soaked and blended lentil.

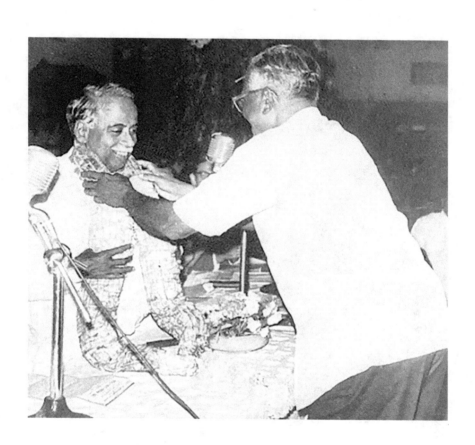

ABOUT THE AUTHOR

June Samuel, in her odyssey, has traveled across the world and finds people endlessly fascinating. She is a physician and counselor. Her medical degree is from Madras Medical College, India, and counseling degree from Tuskegee University, USA. She lives with her family in Alabama, USA.

CPSIA information can be obtained
at www.ICGtesting.com
Printed in the USA
BVHW060745300622
640819BV00014B/1012

9 781685 262631